The New and Bigger What Am I?

A Hawai'i Animal Guessing Game

Written by Daniel Harrington

Illustrated by Susan Brandt

Mutual Publishing

ISBN-13: 978-1939487-54-4
Library of Congress Control Number: 2015944066

First Printing, September 2015
Second Printing, August 2017

Mutual Publishing, LLC
1215 Center Street, Suite 210
Honolulu, Hawai'i 96816
Ph: 808-732-1709 / Fax: 808-734-4094
Email: info@mutualpublishing.com
www.mutualpublishing.com

Printed in Taiwan

I swim in the ocean and dive deep down.
Sometimes I make clicking and squeaking sounds.
When I jump from the water, I spin in the air,
and, by the way, I don't have any hair.

What am I?

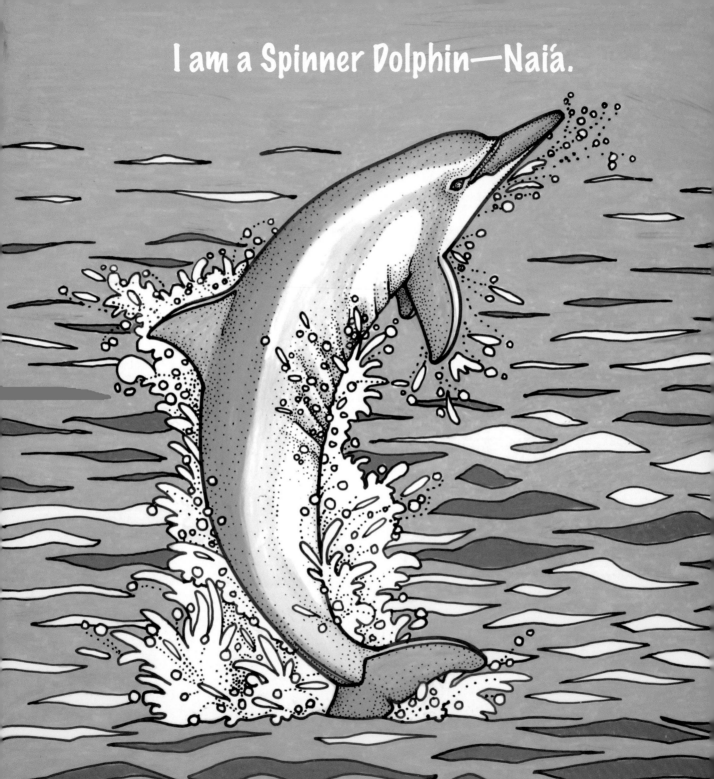

I am a Spinner Dolphin—Naiá.

I am a bird that flies very high.
As I soar across the Hawaiian sky,
I dive into the ocean to catch a squid.
And the feathers on my tail are long and red.

What am I?

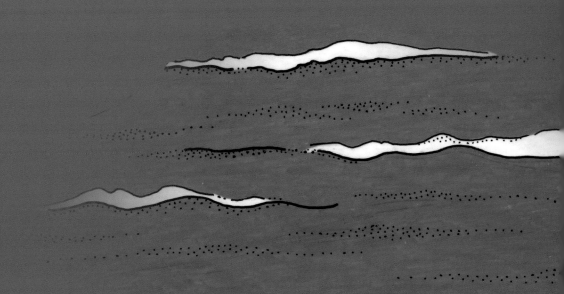

I am a Red-Tailed Tropicbird—Koaʻe ʻUla.

I am green, and I am really quite small.
You may have seen me walk up walls
or across the ceiling upside down.
I am very small, but I make a loud sound.

What am I?

I am a Gecko—
Móʻo ʻAlā.

You might be able to see me from the beach.
When I jump from the water it's called a breach.
Look for my spout shooting way up high
like a fountain of water into the sky.

What am I?

I am a Humpback Whale—Koholā.

I am green, and I swim around in the sea
looking for food near the coral reef.
And one more thing that I should tell,
on my back I have a very hard shell.

What am I?

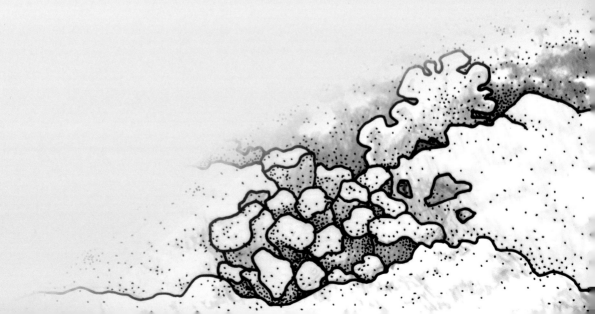

I am a Hawaiian Green Sea Turtle—Honu.

I am a tall bird with long, pink legs,
and I like to eat fish, worms, and crabs.
I search for food in fields of taro,
and my neck is black and very narrow.

What am I?

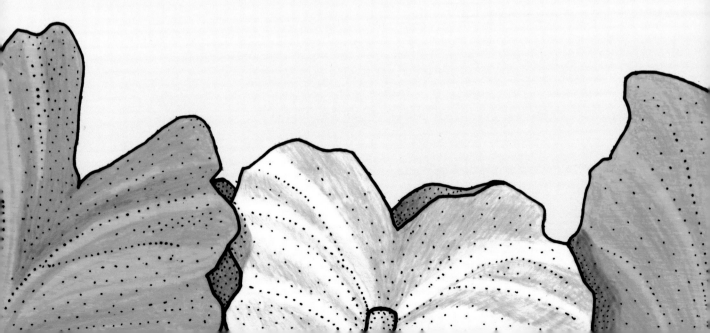

I am a Black-Necked Stilt—Aeʻo.

My name is heavenly, and I like to swim.
My body is narrow and very thin.
And since I am a fish, I also have fins.
Now if you can guess my name, you win.

What am I?

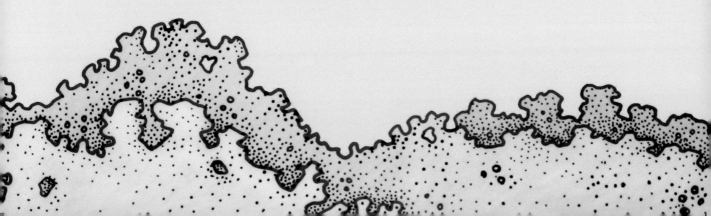

I am an Angelfish.

I have whiskers, and I am really quite round,
And I make a sort of barking sound.
I like to lie on the beach to sleep and rest,
because sleeping on the beach is the best.

What am I?

I am a Monk Seal—ʻĪlioholoikauaua.

My feathers are a beautiful golden brown,
and my whistle is a clear, sweet sound.
I feed on insects, flowers and leaves,
and run on the grass with bursts of speed.

What am I?

I am a Pacific Golden Plover—Kōlea.

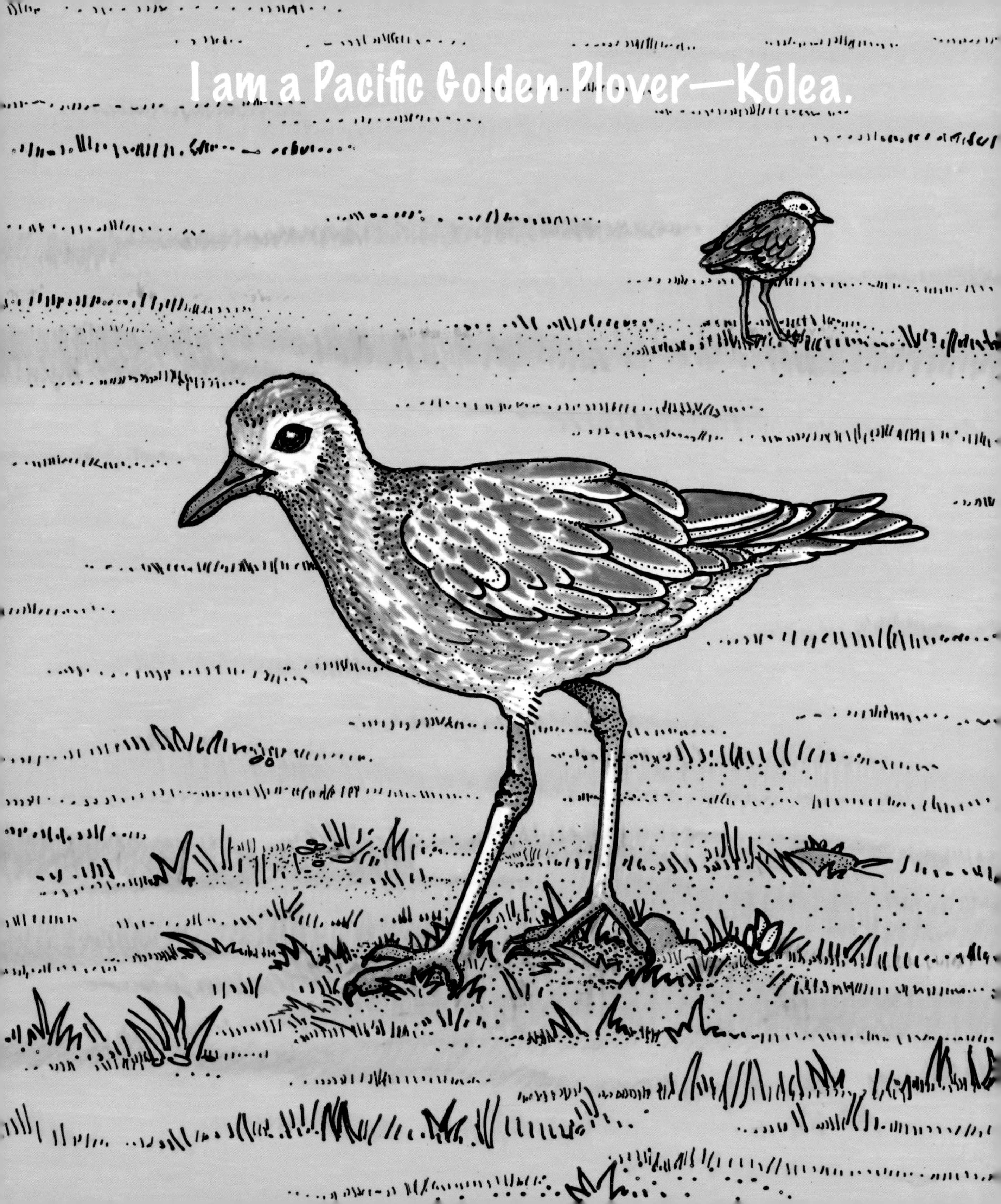

I am one of the fastest fish in the sea,
and my nose is long and as sharp as can be.
Yes, I am known for my pointed snout.
When you see it you might let out a shout.

What am I?

I am a Swordfish—Aʻu.

I am named after a great Hawaiian king.
You may have seen me flutter my wings,
which are reddish-orange and lined with black.
I might fly away, but then I fly back.

What am I?

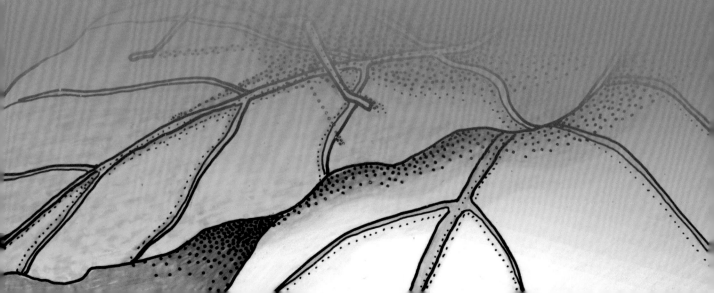

I am a Kamehameha Butterfly—Lepelepe-o-Hina.

At night I soar silently through moonlit skies.
My body is brown, and I have two yellow eyes
that see well in the dark when I am looking for food,
which I dive down and grab if it looks any good.

What am I?

I am a Hawaiian Owl—Pueo.

I walk sideways on the beach at night.
If people are near, I hide out of sight.
But it is easy to tell where I have just been,
because I leave behind little piles of sand.

What am I?

I am a Crab—Pāpaʻi.

I have blue blood, three hearts, and no bones.
And if I lose an arm, a new one will grow.
I have no problem picking things up,
because my arms are lined with suction cups.

What am I?

I am an Octopus—He'e.

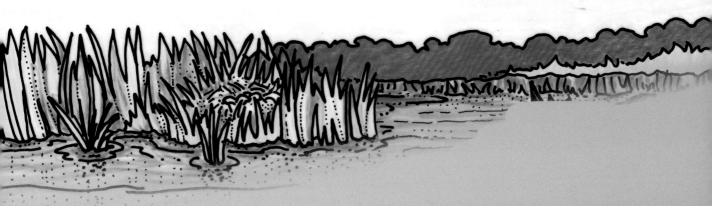

My body is brown and my head is green.
I build my nest right next to a stream.
My legs are orange and so are my feet,
and I search for insects and snails to eat.

What am I?

I am a Hawaiian Duck—Koloa.

I have wings but I am not a bird.
My name is a common baseball word.
I like to hang upside down at night.
If you are alone, I might give you a fright.

What am I?

I am a Hawaiian Bat—ʻŌpeʻapeʻa.

My body is yellow, and I eat fish and shrimp.
And my name is like a musical instrument.
I lure in my prey with a barbel on my chin,
and my mouth is like a vacuum pulling food in.

What am I?

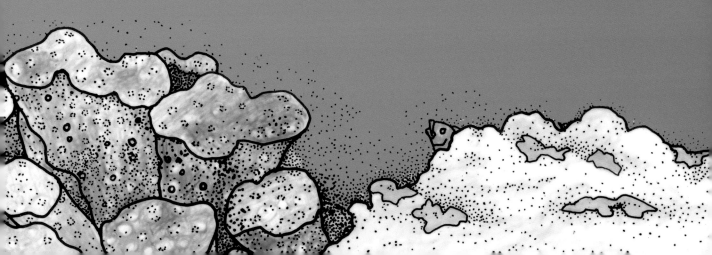

I am a Trumpetfish—Nūnū.

I am brown on top and white underneath.
And I build my nest with twigs and leaves.
I soar through the sky to the highest heights,
then dive down fast when I'm catching mice.

What am I?

I am a Hawaiian Hawk—'Io.

I am born at the top of a mountain stream,
then the water carries me down to the sea.
In the ocean, I grow bigger and then I return
to swim up the same stream where I was born.

What am I?

I am a Hawaiian Goby—ʻOʻopu.

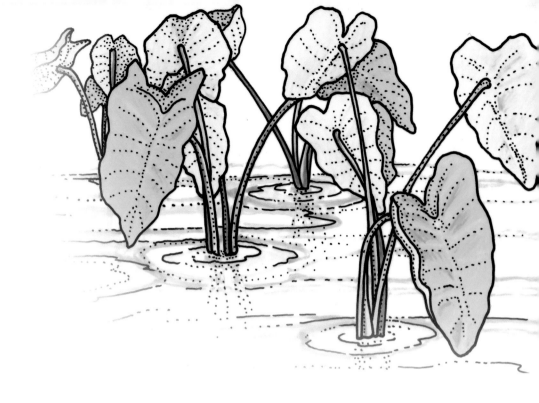

My body is black and as plump as can be,
and my red beak might be the first thing you see.
I search for food in the taro patches.
And I eat whatever my red beak catches.

What am I?

I am a Moorhen—ʻAlae ʻUla.

Under the leaf of a tree I hide
to catch what is on the other side.
My body is yellow, and if you look a while,
you will see my black and red smile.

What am I?

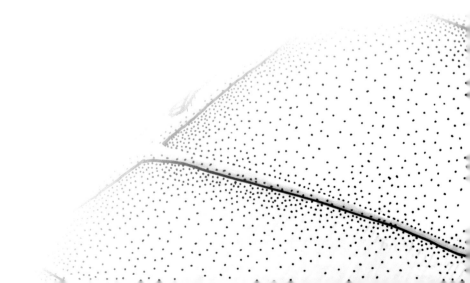

I am an insect with delicate wings.
My front legs are used for catching things.
If you look very close, you might be surprised
when you see my two very strange-looking eyes.

What am I?

I am a Dragonfly—Pinao.

My neck is black and striped with brown.
You may have seen me flying around
or walking by a river and over a rock.
When a group of us fly, it is called a flock.

What am I?

I am a Hawaiian Goose—Nēnē.